Advent
to
Advent

A Spiritual Journey

Denny Bradbury

Published by New Generation Publishing in 2020

First Edition

ISBN: 978-1-80031-893-9

www.newgeneration-publishing.com

New Generation Publishing

This collection is dedicated to my family and friends who have encouraged and helped me to bring this to a conclusion. To all those who believed in me and helped me to try to reach a wider audience, thank you.

Introduction

This book of poetry was inspired over many years by a need for spiritual poems that encapsulate important events in the church's calendar. It is through my own desire, alongside that of others who have asked me, to compose poetry for these annual stepping stones. Sometimes the inexplicable can best be voiced in verse as this can make it seem more accessible or join those who are united in their non understanding of a very difficult world.

The church year follows a story of hope and anticipation through miracles, parables and then betrayal and death. An ordinary tale perhaps except where faith steps in and offers resurrection and new life, then it becomes something rather more wonderful. The first section of this book marks the annual journey followed from Advent through to Pentecost and then on to Harvest and Remembrance. Finally as we approach Advent once more we celebrate Christ the King.

Saints and their lives hold real fascination as they veer from fact to fiction and back again with embroidery and tweaking in between. Whatever the truth the stories are intriguing. The final play has been performed locally and is an Old Testament tale. It is a celebration of welcome for the stranger alongside some historical 'scene setting' for the New Testament stories yet to come. Whatever your faith or if you have none at all I hope that you find something in this collection to help you through times in your life, both good and bad, and celebrate with me some amazing relationships that inform and shape our lives.

Part Three contains one short play (approximately 20 to 30 minutes running time).

The images used in this book have all been photographed by me and include my favourite oak tree and images from my local church, St Peter and St Paul, Wingrave, Buckinghamshire.

Denny Bradbury

Part One - Through the Year

Advent	*England*
Christmas Eve	*Celebration for the Eve of Christmas*
Christmas Day	*Christmas Quatrain*
Epiphany	*i) Different Journeys - Same Star*
	ii) Don't Lose the Star
Candlemas	*Purify and Pray*
Ash Wednesday/	
Lent	*Ash Wednesday*
	A Personal Journey Forty Days
Palm Sunday	*Crossing of Paths*
Good Friday	*i) Good Friday*
	ii) To Judas
Easter Sunday	*Easter Awakening*
Ascension	*i) Journey to Mount Olivet*
	ii) Thoughts on Ascension
Pentecost	
Trinity Sunday	*HolyTrinity*
Lammas	*Lammas*
Harvest Festival	*Harvest*
All Saints' Day	*All Saints' Day*
Remembrance Sunday	*i) God Knows Who*
	ii) One Hundred Years
	iii) At the Eleventh Hour
Christ the King	*King of Kings*

Part Two – Saints

Part Three - Play

Part One
Through the Year

Advent

Advent – England

Advent in November
ninth month of the Roman year
for us it is a gloomy time
wet mud and little cheer

that is until the last weekend
before December reigns
when Advent comes inviting
us to sing with hope again.

A time that's full of angels
on wings of pure delight
with tales of good news coming
words shining in full flight.

Candles' light reminds us
of people who have gone
but left with us a challenge
To believe in God's own son.

The journey of Joseph and Mary
astride a donkey, kind;
a difficult and lonely road
we should bear them in mind.

The coming of a saviour
the anticipated sight
of a gift for all the world
a little boy of Light!

Christmas Eve

Celebration for the Eve of Christmas

The donkey looked on as the archangel came
she wondered why Mary, young girl of pure name,
was scared by a sight as God sent her His word
that she was to carry the Light of the world.

She had been steady, right from a foal
revelling in the love of a girl;
she pulled and carted till work came to an end
then waited for Mary most steadfast of friends.

They frolicked and played together at eve
knowing the two of them never would leave
the other alone until both were old
looking out for each other in winter's harsh cold.

Such an old story both of anguish and pain,
then after a while comes the joy once again;
a baby is born which brings such great pleasure
for Mary relief and love in full measure.

For Joseph the knowledge that fatherhood brings
responsibility with great love in all things;
anticipation of growing and teaching his son
all that he knows when the day's work is done.

This birth though was special, it came with a star,
shepherds and wise men they journeyed so far
to kneel and to welcome this most wondrous child
a present, so precious, from God to the world.

Humble donkey who carried Mary so true
never stumbled with girl dressed in virginal blue;
she served her pure mistress with love and delight
so we pray and we sing for our Saviour this night!

Christmas Day

Christmas Quatrain

Celebrate God's gift of joy
above the transient broken toy,
Dedicate these festive days
to loving kindness in countless ways.

Epiphany

Different Journeys - Same Star

Walking through the woods with soft decay under my feet,
winter trees bare and silent stand as they have for centuries,
lean Labrador snuffles in the undergrowth loving new smells,
fallen branches lay like bones stripped bare by hungry deer.

Three men travel across the desert with the cold of night deep
within their bones, they do not notice as they lift their
eyes to the sky assiduously following the star that has led them
from their books and reckonings, their homes and comfort.

I look to the stars for life's meaning, the often drab and
dreary places wherein we try to find a reason for so much that
is unexplained and often inexplicable to me in my
lack of understanding, I so want the story to be true!

Yet long ago those three wise and mysterious men thought
that they knew the meaning and went through danger to
find the answers to a myriad questions and worship at the feet
of one so small, but who brought Light to their existence.

Do the trees know what we do not? Does my dog suspect the
truth? Do we have to know what we cannot prove?
Is not feeling the Spirit enough? Can the Light not shine
brightly so that we shield our eyes and just trust and believe?

I wonder!

The Magi journeyed to find their King;
My journey too is within my own imagining;
But wherever we find the Truth and the Light
It is our reality and that is all we need to know.

Don't Lose the Star

"Don't lose the star" the wise man said
"don't lose our guiding light"
they'd travelled far away from home
on promise of the sight;
a wondrous Light to them that meant
the answer to their quest.

Herod sought to lure them back
In this he did his best
to make them think that he was good
and wanted to behave
as any other at the feet
of Him who'd come to save.

They travelled on but all did dream
of angels and their song
"Do not return to this harsh land
that king will do great wrong."

First Sage had grown so weary
"I'm tired and out of sorts"
The second man had ridden far
"I'm sad beyond all thought"

The third exotic king then said
"We'll stop awhile and think"
He reigned in his loyal mount
"I know we're on the brink"
"We lose faith now and everything
will stay in darkest night,
rest my friends then by this star
go on to greater Light."

The first Sage felt into his cloak
found frankincense therein
he then was calm and understood
the Spirit deep within.

The second King was fretful,
his gift was hard to give
for myrrh had portents difficult
the child would die to live.

Meanwhile the third man of the group
stood looking at the sky
so dark yet shining bright as day
was the star they were steering by.

His gift of gold was mighty,
His gift of gold was pure,
He knew that this was God he sought
He'd never been more sure.

They came upon a humble home,
strangers stood on guard;
they'd taken in the family
whose journey had been hard.

The three wise men then knelt in prayer
they were received with grace
their journeying was now fulfilled
to gaze on such a face.

Candlemas

Purify and pray

Present the child and purify,
purify and pray;
pray that all the prejudice
leaves us from this day.

Light a candle, light one more,
light a thousand strong;
so we can see in darkest night,
and right will conquer wrong.

Present the child and purify,
purify and pray;
pray that all injustices
are broken down today.

Light a candle, light one more,
light can do no wrong;
it lights the darkest corner,
illuminates our song.

The song of hope and faith and love;
The song of praise and awe,
that through winter's bitter cold
the sun will rise once more.

Present the child and purify
purify and pray;
pray as we hold our candles high
that all will find their way.

Forty Days

Forty days and forty nights
now that's a long, long time
to be without, with no one near
to cheer you with a rhyme,
or sunny smile or cheerful chat,
such loneliness can kill
the isolated; who are left
may feel that burden still.

But Jesus in his hour of need
sought solace from his Dad,
who gave him strength to carry on
though hunger drove him mad;
but not enough to listen to
the voices in his head
that told him he could aspire,
he turned away instead.

Just as we might also seek
the comfort of the Light,
that brightens each and every day
so we are safe from fright.
Fear drives too many down the path
the wrong and thorny way;
let us rejoice in company
and welcome in the stray.

For who knows where,
why, what or when
we may that stranger be
Let hope and faith open the door
ask Jesus in for tea.

Ash Wednesday

ash marks my forehead
communion wafer lies heavy on my tongue
beginning of Lent

giving up for weeks
no comforting food to stem the feelings of loss
Lent has begun

Lent (continued)
A Personal Journey

2nd

March winds blow cruel cold
how was that first journey into mountain bleakness no
comfort there

Giving up - giving up
what will bring the edge of sacrifice to my pampered life
I truly wonder

3rd

Sorrowful leaden sky
reflects the sadness in my heart at what has passed
I fear the present

In stark mountains hidden
cold seeping into His body and His tortured mind
He surely wondered

4th

I feel the rhythm of denial
the sun shines on my meagre protest which is all I can manage
suffering - what suffering

Wandering in the wilderness
weight of humanity on your thin shoulders ridden by doubt
that is suffering

5th

Guilt covers my face
I've fallen from the tree of grace as quickly as I climbed
spirit is weak

There was no guilt back then
how can you fall from God's grace when you are God
His own suffering

6th

The world is in a winter
a winter state of mind where people bomb the innocent
no glory there to find

how can those victims realise
the presence of a god who doesn't interfere at all
no glory there - no doubt

7th

Today is much more hopeful
the news is still more dire but somehow through the misery
I feel the heavenly quire

we must keep up the battle
to fight in our own way for human rights and justice
for this I pray

8th

Were there birds in the mountains
did they stay by your side did they sing songs of hopefulness
did they help stem the tide

was it here that you saw
the lost lamb of your heart protected it loved it
never to part

9th

How do we merit love in such measure
are our sacrifices really enough even if we feel the pain
a lifetime through

eternal joy eternal pain
these are the mainsprings of loss and of gain love and its minions
a lifetime through

10th

After we've settled the pain and the loss
we just give our love and send it out from the cross
uplifting love

falter we may get up and get on
no use in dwelling on what might have been we need to have
more
universal love

11th

As you trod the stony path
how did you react when stones not bread accompanied
your every waking hour

did not the bird song
nor the bleat of goat and lamb alike keep you focussed on the
moment
when treachery would strike

12th

Did you hear your Father's voice
borne in softly on the wind did you imagine Him with you
in your soul and in your mind

were you fearful in your way
that this was all too much to bear turning stones into your bread
did it seem you might go there

were you ever in some doubt
as to the task that you were set breathing mountain dust and dirt
did giving in occur to you

13th

I can't believe you wavered then
it all makes sense to me that you were ever steadfast true
if only we could see

How much more the sacrifice
of the lenten journey means if you lead us to the top
where we rest in God's safe arms

14th

Feelings of guilt
I am overwhelmed by the myriad ways I have transgressed
need to regain proportion

Focus on Mary
did Jesus take his leave of her as He withdrew to momentous
domain
how did she bear it

15th

Morning fog lifts
revealing the stillest of days time for standing thinking
absorbing nature

my fog also disappears
how must we go on we fight for what is right tolerance justice
love for all
it is the only way

16th

Kith and kin
so important to us just so the family that Jesus left behind
how did they feel

Joseph and his children
father and siblings to God what an honour what a burden
what a mystery

17th

Simple fishermen
eleven men left to wonder why their friend and leader had gone
without them

how could they begin
to understand the enormity of the position that Jesus was in
dying to live

18th

A concept so difficult
an idea that we find too heavy to contemplate
in the depth of our minds

that living and breathing
we function just so eating and working and loving
onward we go

19th

But tell us we die
then live once more in the bosom of God
shakes us to the core

the life we are given
through love and desire is made much more precious
by heavenly choir

20th

I once met an angel
so softly she came that before I had noticed
she'd gone left no name

but I know it was heaven
sent her to see that I needed a guardian
there she was just for me

21st

The image of Jesus
seared into my mind as a tower of strength sometimes angry
but kind

How would He feel
if He came here today become suffused with such sorrow
would He weep

22nd

Was Mary dry eyed
as she waited for Him her first born to come down the
mountain again
did she cry

How did Joseph then comfort
the woman he knew as his wife but the handmaid of God too
did he weep

23rd

He probably did the thing that he could
he made her a keepsake out of hard olive wood
it was love

love that kept all of them
deep in the well of loneliness/happiness how can we tell love
will survive

24th

I spoke to my oak tree
it grows large by the field I walk then I stand and speak softly
I hear the noises around

no rustle of leaves yet
its branches now zing with sap rising calling the birds to its
form it stands there yet

25th

If only we could know
what the trees have seen throughout the centuries they stand
and become wise

Perhaps we should stand more often
listen to the earth as it tells its story of survival and torment at
human hands

26th

Did you wake up cold
stiff and hungry from your nightly prayers did the stones
bend to your form
were you afraid

were there any signs of spring
did nature offer just one morsel of colour in a flower
to give hope

27th

I see the blackthorn
flowers so white they hurt your eyes in their wakening from the
dull brown hedge

small oases of green
hedgerows coming to life after a winter of retreat and renewal
glorious

28th

Today I saw a kingfisher
what a delight of colour in a drab post winter world
where is the sun

hiding behind storm clouds
rain gives us such a green countryside we should be grateful
we will be patient

29th

O light a flame within my heart
I am ready
truly ready

all doubts pushed to one side as I am overtaken by music
it was if an angel choir sang this morning

30th

Stand still and listen
what do you hear - the sound of peace or does misery draw near
hounding your senses

stand still and look
with all that you have be aware of the beauty
surrounding you be glad

31st

Did Mary stand with Joseph
with her children by her side trying to decipher the enigma in
their lives

How did their first born son
become so difficult to read alone within the mountains now
but just what did he need

32nd

He wanted them to understand
His time on earth so short but what a journey what a life
just miracles to share

just miracles and prayer and angst
wisdom from the heart wisdom mixed with love and faith but
mostly love

33rd

Passion - what are we to make of it
Passion Sunday - if we do nothing then does that make it
meaningless

Meaningless only
if the last person standing does nothing and walks away
someone will stand up someone must

34th

An owl swooped by
early morn in every way a gift the steadfast sun but bitter wind
April in the shires

the long drear winter
no snow just damp and dull and blackly cloudy sky
we long for warmth

35th

My favourite oak tree
still no green just a thickening of its branches as it prepares
for awakening

just as the disciples
didn’t know what they were waiting for
but it was Awakening

36th

Daffodil yellow filled the eye
now they have gone so transitory but so beautiful
no doubt why

everything has its life span
usefulness and beauty fill the hours while we live work and love
it is the world's way

37th

Cold cold sun of Holy Week
bitter wind blows from the east making us wait for joy
we wait yet

Warmth of a smile
a friendly face or a kind word and the biting wind
lessens to nothing

38th

In these Islands
battered by Atlantic storms prey to capricious bitter easterly winds
we are driven by the weather

Today is dull and cold
and so are my thoughts as they turn forward to dreams
of summer and warmth

39th

The wait is almost over
it has been a long forty days and nights
how much more for a soul

wandering in the mountains
the cold nights and relentless days leading Him to pain
and death

40th

The wait is over
the day has come it is a bleak day but the darkness of the hour
will be transient

The sun will rise again
as we trust and believe
it will be glorious

Palm Sunday

Crossing of Paths

Two men of stature rode that day
one from the west in bright array
his soldiers guarding him left and right
as he rode on to further delight

Abba - Father the children sang
as his last journey there began

Another rode in dusty robe
from east he came on palm strewn road
his followers let their spirits rise
seeing people's passion fill their eyes

Abba - Father the children danced
as his disciples watched entranced

Pilate rode to greatest acclaim
he thought that all would know his name
a Prefect so cruel he ruled with iron
his aim to crush the people of Zion

Abba - Father the children sang
as his last journey there began

He rode and waved and smoothed his mount
surrounded by people too many to count
he knew this was just part of his story
until he rose from the grave to glory

Abba - Father the children danced
as his disciples watched entranced

Pilate aware of crowds in the square
thought that they had gathered there
for him their leader their Roman lord
but no as he entered he was ignored

Abba - Father the children sang
as his last journey there began

Jesus rode on to tumultuous cheer
the square was filled with his followers there
he looked and saw Pontius Pilate's ire
round his own feet was a sweeter choir

Abba - Father the children danced
as his disciples watched entranced

Two men who rode on that fateful day
one held earthly power to sway
but the one who sat on the lowly steed
would die and rise in our hour of need

Abba - Father the children sang
as his long journey there began

Good Friday

A blessed day for Christians all
the cross as symbol stops the fall
of man to man when war is raged
unbidden sees the devil caged.

We all can see in God we trust
but contrition is a must
no use deciding who we are
then go and pray to falling star.

It is a certain fact that we
will fall and hurt and wounded be
but hope springs ever in the breast
so moving on we do our best.

Good quiet solemn contemplation
on our knees in deep oblation
then we rise with heart and mind
feeling better thoughtful kind.

To Judas

Looking back o'er space and time
just how does Judas feel?

Two thousand years have come and gone,
does it still seem real?

He did what he was guided to,
he did what fate required;

they paid him to betray his friend,
is his spirit tired?

Hanged and laid, no ceremony,
in potter's field to stay;

his mortal bones at rest awhile
thence to dust, decay.

What if he hadn't given in
to pressure from the scribes?

What if he'd stuck by Jesus?
How then the turn of tides?

We wouldn't have Good Friday,
we wouldn't have the Lamb,

there would be no arising,
no mourning at the tomb.

Jesus needed Judas;
God used him in his plan,

resurrection, hope, and love
pivot on this man.

We had to have the darkness
that we might have the Light.

I hope his spirit's easy now
So Judas, it's all right.

Easter Sunday

Easter Awakening!

Can it be true? Can it really be true?
Sometimes its hard to believe.

Cynical century filled so with gadgets
cynical times laden with trash
that beams out from screens
never sleeping or silent
pictures bombard us
endlessly screaming

"Don't believe, don't believe!
It's all rubbish, just dreaming".

Cold darkness of Friday
seeps into our veins
chills us, reminds us of
Jesus' pains.

But Easter, now Easter
is full of such glory;
He's risen, He's risen.
Oh hear such a story
of good trumping evil,
of light over shade,
of sacrifice, goodness,
thank heavens,
He came.

Ascension

Journey to Mount Olivet

They journeyed forth, those who were left,
for three long years they'd tried;
they ministered and healed and prayed,
lost heart the day He died.

When Mary said He wasn't dead,
but risen from the tomb,
she told of angels waiting there
whose words dispelled her gloom.

Now He was come among them
He led them to the hill,
to the chosen mount of Olivet,
the day was calm and still.

He told them of the holy ghost
who would baptise with fire
and then they could go out with God
heal souls, teach to inspire.

Most were simple fisherfolk
who had seen mighty power
from He who walked among them
now was His crowning hour.

Two angels came on wings of cloud
they took Him up with them
to sit with God and reign supreme
in the glorious light of heaven.

Thoughts on Ascension
(Jesus considers)

My work here now is done,
although only begun;
this man can do no more,
but God can, that is sure.

These men have been my friends,
good hearted to the end,
perhaps confused and weak
still no others did I seek;
but many came to me,
and proved their constancy;
those women who saw truth
within my ministry,
were ceaseless in their care,
and suffered much for me.

One disciple was to blame
but I love him all the same.

My angels wait upon
the cloud of woe-begone,
now I go back to see
what heaven will be for me;
my father three in one
of whom I am the son,
our spirit is yet free
to comfort where she please.

Pentecost
(Shavuot - anniversary of the giving of the Torah - wheat harvest)

’Twas Joel that prophesied, told them the deal
with God and his spirit before those that kneel;
after an era of the darkest of hours,
they would be chosen and granted such powers;
the spirit divine would land in their minds
and send them to places as far as the winds
could carry them over some very rough seas,
to go among those who were sorely in need.

And the young shall have visions

while the old dream their dreams!

They’d come to a gath’ring to celebrate wheat
weeks after passover restricted their meat,
apostles surrounded by people who sought
a sign of salvation, the meeting was fraught;
consumed as they stood with a heavenly fire
that filled them with words like an angelic quire,
the twelve started speaking in terms understood
by each one who looked on for spiritual food

And the young shall have visions

while the old dream their dreams!

Apprehensive, astonished, suffused with joy
the twelve knew their calling and they would employ
all of the teachings of their friend who had gone
and told them so many times what he had done.
This was their journey, they were chosen for this,
To teach and to suffer a bleak kind of bliss,
But we remember them, by symbol and word,
And act as if we were there praising the Lord.

And the young shall have visions

while the old dream their dreams!

Holy Trinity

'How can it be that we are one?
How can we make it real?
The thought that each of us is whole
but part of an ideal.'

God thought of how to put it,
Jesus raised a smile,
the Holy Spirit paced and flew
then sat and thought a while.

God said to Jesus, "This is how
we'll make them understand,
You go down and do our work
and suffer like a man.

Our Holy Spirit will be there
to get you through the pain
then after all the troubles
you come back to us again.

You know my son you're all of me
as I am all of you,
our spirit is our binding love
and we know who is who.

The human race will take a time
to understand our bond;
millennia will pass away;
you know I'm awfully fond

of those who try and try again
to solve the mystery
but then when all is said and done
we are the Trinity".

Lammas

Bless the harvest and mill the wheat
then take the bread back home to eat.

Give thanks for wind, frost, sun and showers
that gave the grain its growing powers

Man shall not live by bread alone!
But food is what we need,
corporeal and spiritual,
both entities must feed.

God given world in which we dwell
is full of wonder, so we tell

our children, and those who will hear,
about God's love that is so clear.

With faith we pray and thank the Lord
for turning ploughshares from the sword!

Harvest

The church is full of fruit and veg
bags and boxes fill the aisles
people rush to groaning seats
anticipatory smiles.

Marrows lie beside the pears,
tomatoes line the altar,
potatoes, beetroot, leeks all tell
of hands that did not falter.

All shapes and sizes, row on row
of produce brought for sharing;
just like the people in the pews
diverse, but all are caring.

They sowed and weeded, stood and watched
as leaves then fruit exploded
into a riot of colour and shape
each as special,
unique as we are,
farmers and gardeners doing their best
to bring forth food so
all can eat
until we are too much replete.

In the midst of plenty
remember the poor,
those who have nothing
but the wolf at the door.

All Saints Day

We pass them by without a word
our daily lives too cluttered
with thoughts prosaic, humdrum, grey,
how beautiful are those who bring love!

We pass them by without a thought,
but they are suffering still,
their eyes are dim, their hair unwashed,
how beautiful are those who bring peace!

If we could only see their soul,
their inner light that shines,
would we then share their agony?
How beautiful are those who bring comfort!

Yet there are those who do not pass
their hearts compassion filled,
hands ready to offer their love,
how beautiful are those who bring joy!

These are the saints around us now,
these are the saintly souls,
they will have their glory sometime where
the Light Eternal glows.

Remembrance

God Knows Who

Poppies still grow
trees yet stand
guardians over a war torn land

spirits long dead
in the ground
corn grows peacefully all around

fields have seen
so much distress
we'll leave them to what they do best

let hedgerows run
wild with rose
as we sit and remember those

for whom there will
be no treat
of apple and blackberry pie to eat

they fought our cause
commend them now
think of white crosses row on row

many have names
some do not
God knows who is in every plot

it matters today
keep in mind
those whom war left far behind

let's live in peace
find a way
to honour, remember, smile and say

heartfelt thanks to
those who fall
for our today they gave their all.

DO THIS IN REMEMBRANCE OF ME

One Hundred Years
(1918 - 2018)

The graveyard where you soldiers sleep,
all tidy in neat rows;
is tranquil, calm, restorative;
your fate, God only knows.

Spring sunshine plays about your stones,
pure white or grey of years,
the morning is a peaceful one,
sad memories bring tears.

War Graves Commission keeps the grass
so carefully its mown,
rest quietly with honour kept,
you stepped up each alone.

The wider world is still at war.
We never get it right,
But while there is still fear and greed
humans will always fight.

One hundred years, one hundred years
since your war was resolved;
but what a world we know today,
of that you are absolved.

So rest in peace with grateful thanks.
We owe you much and more.
I'm sorry though we're still at odds
since you have fought your war.

Your graves have peace, what irony!
No wonder that I grieve
to think of all you lost and gave.
So now I take my leave.

At the Eleventh Hour

Two comrades stand alone and proud,
they keep their vigil to the end,
silent on things they saw and did,
their minds are fixed on friends now dead.

Children sleep while the poppies grow
deep red in fields of green and gold,
perhaps they will grow up to know
the debt they owe to those of old.

Stand tall and proud amid the throng,
silently let the teardrops fall,
let not their lives be shed for nought,
we fix our minds on bugler's call!

Christ the King

King of Kings

(Stir up Sunday)

Stir up the fruit of all the land
take the spoon and give a hand
the King is here
his feast is clear
no one goes hungry
none need fear.

Stir up the grain of golden corn
miller worked from night til morn
the king has come
his crown adorns
a noble head
on shoulders broad.

Stir up molasses, silken wine
mix up your cup of drink divine
break up the bread
pass it on piece by piece
crumb by crumb.

Stir up the love all hands employ
boundless is God's cup of joy
take just one sip
its all you need
The King of Kings
your soul will feed.

Part Two
Saints

PSALMS
Prayer

St Swithun

With the ear of kings, public acclaim,
Bishop of Winchester, humble mien,
honest and fervent in loving God,
stony but straight was the road he trod.

The miller's bridge spanned the Itchen wide,
his faithful clerics walked by his side,
he greeted his flock as he passed their way,
whilst humility held pride at bay.

They laid him with care in peasant earth,
unmarked was his grave as was his birth;
then the fervour of sainthood began,
the transformation of saint from man.

His mortal remains were disinterred
with post mortem honour over conferred;
his body was ripped and taken to town
where he was buried with greater renown,

but not before his finger went west
his leg and his head torn from the rest;
miracles followed wherever these went
although from his resting place he was rent.

Carried across the bridge he knew well
while churches all tolled the mourning bell,
the heavens opened, the skies grew dim,
alarmed the people were scared for him.

No light in the gloom as he passed by,
genuine mourners started to cry,
they knew he wanted his humble field
The Bishops and such, poor faith revealed.

Such a storm then soaked each pate
many believed they'd met their fate
river banks bursting on many leas
healing began with men on their knees

He's rested since with a greater Light,
his earthly remains well out of sight,
yet still people now, centuries gone
tell this tale, so his legend lives on.

The Call

Mother Julian! Mother Julian!
I don't know your name
the one that your mother would call
as you wandered away from your home
in the grip of your holy enthral.

As you sat looking out at the blue
of the sky be it daytime or night
were you always convinced of your goal
did you instinctively know what is right
was yours always a pure childlike soul?

Did God's voice on the wind or the tide
gently slide in with delight
and rock you with thoughts so divine
you said, 'Now I'm for an Anchorite
I know the course that is mine'

Was it simple for you, did you doubt
were you ever tempted to sin?
When children bullied and fought
were you there on the edge looking in
thinking violence will all come to nought?

I hope that you gave up some gritty
childhood pleasures and joys
that you threw sticks and muddied the water
and you cried over old broken toys
wishing to stay evermore as a daughter

freezing time that was precious and good
but then you discovered your Father
in churches so simple and plain
that you walked away from your family
a much greater Passion to gain.

How proud and how sad was your mother
when you donned the linen pure
the mark of your face in her memory
full of light and conviction so sure
holy work the one truth in your story.

Do I envy you the faith that was riven
so deep in your brilliant mind?
Shall I ever be even so true
to a tenth of what you left behind?
Only God knows, but maybe I do.

St Cuthbert of Lindisfarne

Aiden the priest taught him God's word
Aiden the priest taught him well
his young mind was turned
his young mind it learned
that prayer is God's way for us all

He stood in the sea all day God to please
he stood in the sea all day
atoning for sin
let nobody in
to his fervent prayer in the bay

He travelled and spoke all day God to please
he travelled and spoke all day
atoning for sin
all comers let in
unshakeable vision held sway

Persuaded by kings and bishops as well
he accepted the Mitre and See
although in his soul
he sought no such goal
but decided to let God's will be

When his time was up as God called him forth
his time had come God to please
he died in the night
he died in the Light
knowing prayers brought his earnest soul ease

A good man and true he mattered to those
who followed his word and pure thought
they made him a saint
on his body no taint
of decay as though death was but nought

the church decided his body was good good
as his word when alive
they honoured his grave
their souls for to save
the crowds knew that his goodness would thrive

Touching his corpse carried high on a bier
people fell on their knees with relief
so many now cured
thousands were lured
to honour pure saintly belief.

Jeremiah - The Long View

He spoke and no-one listened
God gave him words to say
his was the voice of reason
but still they turned away.

The people were all mighty
their arrogance was great,
they set themselves to kingdoms
and God was so irate.

His prophet, Jeremiah,
tried hard to make them see
but death and mass destruction
were God's own mastery.

King Nebuchadnezzar
from Babylon he came,
God sent him to his city
he battled and found fame.

He took away the good folk,
Jeremiah one of these,
this earthly king took pity
on the plight of refugees.

God left the bad to seek the world
for centuries to roam
until they saw the true path
then they could journey home.

Jeremiah kept on preaching,
he spoke of figs and such,
good shepherds with the bad ones,
it didn't matter much.

Forsaken by his people
in lands so far away
he strove for their repentance
through parables and plays.

Meanwhile there were false prophets
who spoke with selfish aim,
they mesmerised the people
all they sought was fame.

Jeremiah took the long view,
he knew that God was cross,
however long it took them
the Jews would not be lost.

They only had to listen
and hear the word of God,
he spoke God's words of wisdom,
'twas a stony road he trod.

Let us sing of Jeremiah,
let us celebrate his woes
then sing and dance forever
with faith that grows and grows.

How Brave Would I Be?

Would I let Jesus in
if he came to my door?
Would I let Jesus in
if He came to save once more?

What guise would cloak his frame?
What tell tale signs to see?
How would I know his name?
Why would He call on me?

How brave would I be then
to see through His disguise
a tramp or holy man
a foe with blazing eyes.

A woman sleekly clad
or trodden down at heel
a child with eyes so sad
someone who needs a meal.

Should I then search within
the gentle soul to find.
We are so quick to wound
but slower cuts to bind.

I should let love take flight
soar above all the pain
God open up my sight
and make me whole again.

Would I let Jesus in
if He came to my door
I like to think I would
for without Him we are poor.

Part Three

One short play that can be used either to engage a congregation in community or to illustrate how we may accept strangers into our lives as we are all loved by God. There is a lot of singing in it which is always a wonderful way to get people to interact and bring joy to the moment.

The play should last approximately 30 minutes but can be shorter if that fits in with worship. I was struck by the story of Ruth when I was taught about it in school. Such loyalty and love was beautiful to me.

Ruth - a story of love

Cast of characters

Ruth
Naomi
Orpah
Boaz
Naomi's cousin
Cousin's wife

Chorus/Narrator

All sing: O God Our help In Ages Past or the organist could just play this hymn tune to set the scene

Introduction by Chorus/Narrator:

We have a little story
set in time long past
about a gentle woman
who left her home in trust.
She followed her dear husband,
her two sons went as well
and with her sons' new wives
in Moab they did dwell.

Disaster fell upon them
the men took ill and died
leaving the stranded women
hopeless and sorely tried;
and so they travelled homeward,
back to where she'd been
part of a wealthy family
her hope was bright and keen.

Scene One

Setting: A dusty road, rocky hillside climbs away into the distance. Naomi and her daughters-in-law shelter from the cold night in a shepherd's stone hut. The only light is from the moon and the stars.

Naomi: My daughters. You have been through so much to stay with me. The road has been long and we have travelled to the edge of the sea. Here we are, a few days from my home and we are tired, cold and hungry. I cannot offer you much hope for a better life when we reach my home village. God seems to have forsaken me, I may even change my name to Misery. I feel so wretched.

She sighs: We are on the border of your land, I love you as my own but now you must and should go back to the homes of your mothers and fathers and leave me. They will offer you shelter and safety. God knows the harvest is poor this year but what they have they will share with you. I must cross the sea to my homeland. It will be hard.

Ruth: We don't want to leave you. What will you do without us?

Orpah: When I married your son you became my mother. I was and am but a girl. It seems a long time since I saw my family, yet I know you speak the truth when you say they will care for me. But how can I leave you like this? You are worn out with worry and travel. We should stay together.

Ruth: *Draws closer to Naomi and shares her shawl with her*

You will be lonely without us. I will be lonely without you. Orpah and I, we have learnt so much from you. She speaks what we both feel. You are my mother now.

Naomi: *Close to tears*

My daughters. We have no man to protect us. I will throw myself on the mercy of my kinsman. I do not know what they will make of you. You are both Moabites and the Jewish people can be...

She searches for the right word

wary of strangers. It is their past that they carry with them, always to unsettle the present.

Orpah: *she is scared by this*

Oh, mother-in-law, what will they do to us?

Naomi: They may not accept you. It will be hard for me but for you, it may be worse. I am going back to where I have land but need a male kinsman to hold the title. Jewish law does not allow that we women own land in our own right. I will have to fight but I have the land to bargain with.

Ruth: Orpah is so much younger than me. Hardly a woman even yet. Perhaps it is the right thing Orpah for you to return to your father's house. Your mother and sisters miss you I know. I saw them standing in their fields as we left, they would welcome you home and you are young enough for a new husband when you are ready. I will not leave Naomi, she and I will journey on. I will work so that we may eat. She will talk to me about her God; who is righteous and magnificent but awesome too. I will put my trust in Naomi's God.

She puts her arm around Orpah's shoulders to comfort her

Let us sleep and in the morning we will do what we have to do.

They lie together in the rude stone hut and keep each other warm. The three women sing a lament.

We are alone within the night of loneliness
(to the tune of Londonderry Air)

We are alone within the night of loneliness
we have each been a wife and now we're through
we have not seen much light amid the darkness
but we have God, he's there for me and you

and this we know that though our lives are difficult
we will get by with every passing day
because we feel the love that is within us all
and so we smile and sleep and in our hearts we pray

Dear God do not let us go through more torment
we will be safe as long as we abide
with honour, gentleness and purest honesty
we each have love and live with God beside

My daughters -
Dear Mother - we will always be together
as long as you both know that we are three
bonded in love, so know that we must leave here
(Naomi) go to your kin and love them as you have loved me
(Orpah) I will go back and find my long lost family
(Ruth) I will not go for you I'll never ever leave

Scene Two

Naomi's Home Village.

Chorus/Narrator

Ruth has stayed with Naomi
she couldn't leave her side,
she knew that the old woman
was lost and hurt inside.
She said she knew that Orpah,
younger by some years,
would be safer going back
their parting - full of tears.

Naomi: We are drawing closer to my village. It looks just as I left it. Look they are harvesting. Let us see what we can do. Ruth, I do hope that you have made the right decision.

Ruth: *Squeezes her mother-in-law's hand*

I told you this morning. Your way is my way. Your land is my land. Your God is my God.

She sees a handsome farmer walking towards them, she hides her face and retreats behind Naomi.

Naomi: Greetings. You may not remember me but I am the widow of Elimelek. You remind me of my cousin, Boaz. I am Naomi.

Boaz: Greetings. I am he, your kinsman. I remember that you all left because of the famine. I hope you found good pasture where you journeyed. We had reports that you lost your menfolk. A tragedy for you all. You have come back to find shelter and care in your homeland?

Naomi: We have. This is my daughter-in-law. Her name is Ruth. She would not leave me. We need to find work so that we may not be a burden.

Naomi looks at Boaz and sees a kind man, she hopes she is not mistaken

Do you know of a kind overseer who will let us do our part?

Boaz: I have men working to bring in the harvest. There is room for one to glean. Your daughter can go behind the men and gather there. Gleaning will feed you well enough. She will come to no harm. I will tell my men.

Ruth: *Still sheltering behind Naomi bows her head in recognition of the honour and protection he has offered.*

Naomi: You are a kind man. I need to find shelter with my kinsmen and seek the solution of the title of my husband's land.

Ruth and Naomi walk on leaving Boaz to go on his way, he does but he looks back intrigued by the younger woman.

Scene Three

Naomi and Ruth have been taken in by Naomi's relatives. It is a temporary solution.

Chorus/Narrator

Naomi finds her kinsmen
they welcome her within,
Ruth they do not cherish
she has a different skin,
marked out as a stranger
the men could be quite cruel
but Boaz was respected
and so they kept their cool.

Naomi: *Sitting with Ruth at the end of a trying day*

Ruth, we need to find a better solution to our problem. Neither of us is as well suited as we could be. Boaz looks at you with favour. He is an honourable man. Go to him tonight, lie at his feet on the threshing floor and cover his feet with your shawl. If he takes you up you will never starve.

Ruth: *She knows what her mother-in-law is asking of her and although not her way she listens to her advice and does as she suggests.*

I will do as you say, Naomi. You ways are my ways, your land is my land, your God is my God and I want to be with you for ever.

The next morning...Boaz calls at the house where Naomi is staying.

Boaz: Naomi, I was surprised by a visitor in the night. All is well. She returns to you unharmed and still protected. You may be surprised when she shows you her shawl, it is full of barley. Take this as a token of my intentions towards her and both your futures. I have called a council of the elders and your husband's cousin is coming and he will be offered the land. He has first claim as you know.

He turns to go then adds

You and Ruth will need to be present.

With a twinkle in his eye he says

Oh and your cousin's wife of many years will also be there.

Scene Four

Village Courtyard where the people gather for the forthcoming transfer of land.

Chorus/Narrator

Boaz sets the deal up
the kinsman takes his place,
the elders meet to chew the cud
they talk with solemn face.

Naomi fears the outcome
of this the legal court,
if her kinsman takes the land
Ruth's future will be fraught.

Boaz: Greetings my people. We have to determine the title of Elimelek's land. Naomi is his widow and therefore your kin. Ruth is her daughter-in-law. Elimelek had title on the land beyond the Grove. You have the right to the land.

Cousin: Yes. I thank you Boaz for such prompt dealing. Knowing that Naomi had returned to us without Elimelek, or her sons, we have discussed the issue of the land and although it is poor land fit only for goats we will take it on out of respect for Elimelek my dearly missed cousin.

The cousin turns to his wife of many years who smiles at him.

Boaz: There is one thing, our law states that you must also take Naomi and Ruth into your household. They go with the land. They will have equal status within the home.

Cousin: *His wife moves to his side and speaks with him quietly. She has stopped smiling*

I am old Boaz, I do not need any more trouble at home.

He takes a deep breath and says

I forfeit the land. You are next in line. You have the honour.

Boaz: I ask the elders here present to acknowledge the right of this transaction. I will take Naomi and Ruth into my home. They will never want for food or shelter again. Theirs has been a hard road. The law allows and so I will marry Ruth.

Naomi and Ruth hug each other.

Chorus/Narrator Boaz was a goodly man
He married lovely Ruth
They had a son called Obed
Siring Jesse and the Truth.
Naomi, well rewarded,
had a grandson to behold
she looked upon him daily
his descendants were foretold.

For Obed begat Jesse
then Jesse in his turn
gave David life and set him
on the path from which we learn.
The story is a clear one
love will rise and each enthral.
Acceptance of the stranger
Jesus lives within us all.

Closing Song - Tune is the Londonderry Air
Lined up are: Boaz, Ruth, Naomi, Cousin, Cousin's Wife - (Chorus line up behind)

Boaz: I have my love, around me are my family
Ruth: I have my love and all my trials are through
Naomi: We each have love and light shines through the darkness
All: We all have God, he's here for me and you
Gesture to the audience

Cousin: And this I know that though my life is difficult
Looks at his wife I will get by while you are by my side
Cousin's Wife: That is so true you'll have my love always
And so we smile and sleep and in my heart I pray
Looks heavenward

All: Dear God we know that you are always here for us
We will be safe as long as we abide
and welcome all to sit and eat and pray with us
For we have you right here with us inside
All touch their hearts

All: Dear God we know that you are always here for us We will be safe as long as we abide
and welcome all to sit and eat and pray with us
Our hearts are full with you right here inside.

(If appropriate encourage the audience/congregation to sing this as well)

The End

www.ingramcontent.com/pod-product-compliance
Ingram Content Group UK Ltd.
Pitfield, Milton Keynes, MK11 3LW, UK
UKHW041845200726
13854UKWH00005BA/2073